A Self-Guided One-Day Itinerary of Local Shops, Historic Sites & Scenic Trails

Mystery Date
Mifflinburg, PA

By Dates in the States

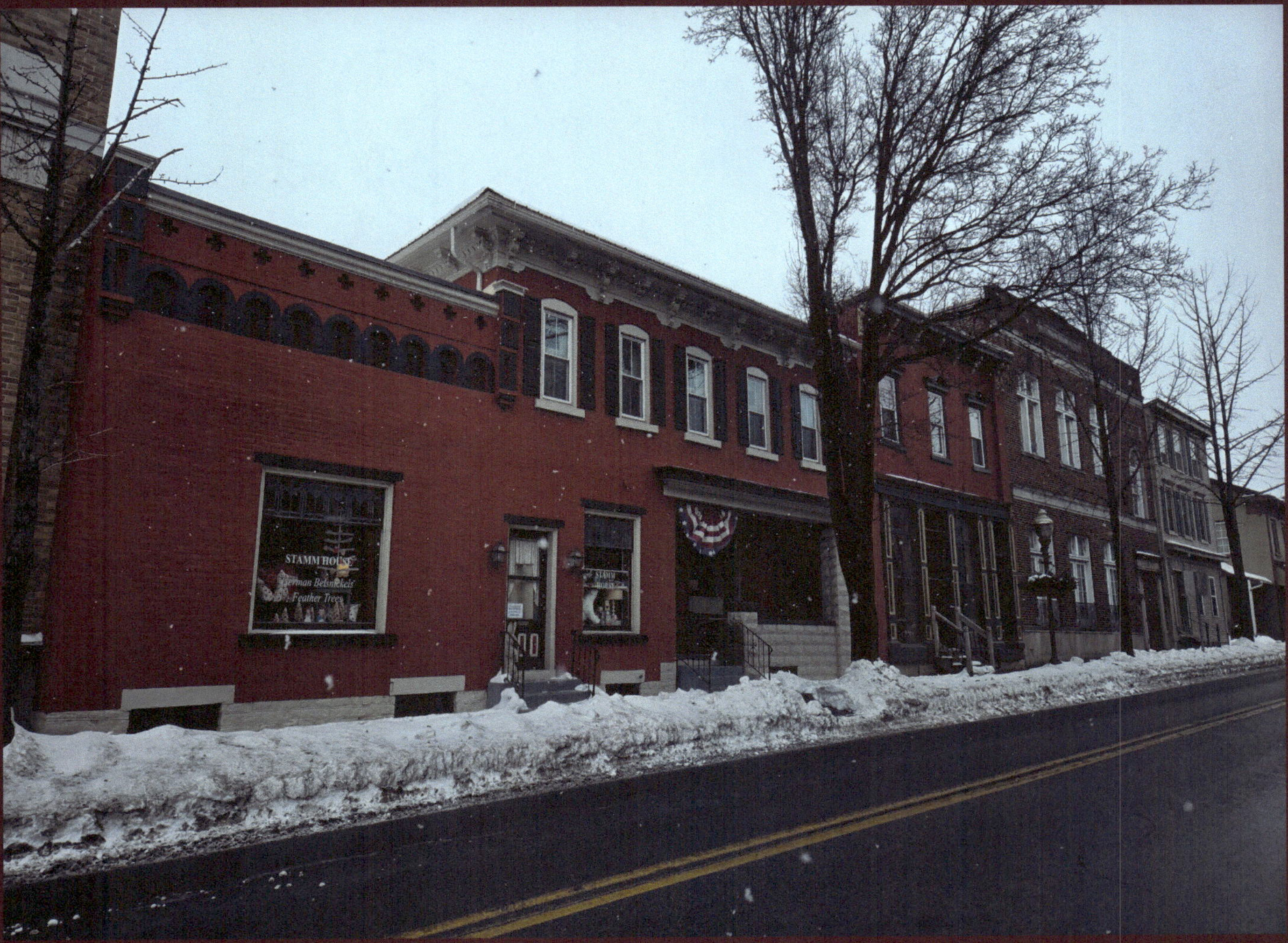

"Our passion is travel, and we want to share our adventures to inspire others to explore the world with their loved ones. Dare to live beyond the box."

Dates in the States

Introduction

Hey there! We're Crystal and Shane, the duo behind Dates in the States, where we share our love for discovering unique adventures, unforgettable moments, and hidden gems across the U.S. Whether you're searching for a fun date idea, a new place to explore, or just a little inspiration, we've got you covered!

Our Mystery Date Books are designed to help couples (and adventurous friends!) shake up their routine and experience the best local spots in a fun, intentional way. Inside, you'll find a curated collection of date ideas. Each one meant to be completed over the course of a single day in a specific neighborhood. All of which are a surprise until you flip the page!

It's like a little challenge to break out of your comfort zone, support local, and make memories that stick. We hope this book helps you laugh more, explore more, and connect more, with each other and with your city. Let the mystery begin!

Here's What To Expect:

In this Mystery City-Date Book, you'll explore the charm of a small Pennsylvania town filled with history, hidden gems, and plenty of opportunities to slow down and look around.

Here's what to expect for your day ahead:

Start your morning with a cozy coffee stop and something freshly baked before wandering through Main Street shops and browsing a favorite thrift store. Step back in time with a stop that highlights the area's craftsmanship and local history, then head out for fresh air with a scenic drive and a peaceful hike, or simply enjoy the views if walking isn't your thing. End the day with a well-earned early dinner and a locally brewed drink, the perfect way to wrap up your date with the city.

1st Stop

IV Coffee Co.
456 Chestnut St.
Mifflinburg, PA 17844

Start your day at IV Coffee Co., a bright, comfortable spot with plenty of room to sit and stay awhile. Beyond coffee and lattes, you'll find energy drinks, teas, lemonades, baked goods and acai bowls. All of which are great options if you're looking for something refreshing or a light bite.

IV Coffee Co. gives you a taste of the town in a welcoming, low-pressure way to begin your date with Mifflinburg, no matter how fast or slow you're moving.

Second Stop

American Rescue Workers Thrift Stor

350 Chestnut St.
Mifflinburg, PA 17844

If you've seen any of our other books, this won't surprise you. We love a good thrift store. And honestly, this one is a favorite. On our many road trips through Mifflinburg, the American Rescue Workers Thrift Store always delivers: great prices and interesting finds. This is a perfect place to wander with your IV Coffee Co. latte in hand and start exploring Main Street.

While you're nearby, there are a few other spots worth popping into, like Stamm House and Artisan Corner Co-op. Take your time, follow what catches your eye, and enjoy getting to know the town at your own pace.

Third Stop
Mifflinburg Buggy Museum
598 Green St.
Mifflinburg, PA 17844

You're in Amish country, and no visit to Mifflinburg feels complete without learning a bit about the buggy. The Mifflinburg Buggy Museum preserves and celebrates the town's 19th-century buggy and sleigh industry, highlighting the craftsmanship that once made this small town a national name in carriage building.

This is a seasonal stop with limited hours, so be sure to check ahead before visiting. If you're lucky enough to come during Buggy Day or a special program, you may see live demonstrations by local artisans who continue these traditional techniques today.

Fourth Stop

DC Coffee & Tea Co.

7 Cedar Green Center.
Mifflinburg, PA 17844

By now you've walked off your first latte, which means it's time for a real meal. DC Coffee & Tea is a solid lunch stop, especially if you're craving something warm and filling. Yes, you can absolutely get another latte, but this is also the place for good soup and sandwiches that actually hold you over.

This is the stop where you can fill up a bit and regroup before the next part of the day. Grab a few snacks to go if something catches your eye, then get ready to head out. Trust us: You'll want fuel up before you continue!

Fifth Stop

Country Pickers

145 E Chestnut St.
Mifflinburg, PA 17844

One thing I love about Pennsylvania is how often you'll stumble into a single building filled with craft, antique, and thrift vendors all under one roof, and Country Pickers is a great example of that. This stop doesn't disappoint.

Take your time walking through aisle after aisle of vendors, each with their own mix of vintage finds, handmade pieces, and unexpected treasures. It's the kind of place where you don't need a plan, just wander, browse, and see what catches your eye. You'll leave with a different perspective on Mifflinburg and maybe a small piece of it to take home with you.

Sixth Stop
Historic Hassenplug Covered Bridge
N 4th St.
Mifflinburg, PA 17844

On your way to the hike, you'll pass through the Historic Hassenplug Covered Bridge. One of Mifflinburg's iconic landmarks. This can be a quick drive-through moment, or you can pull over and take a few minutes to snap photos and appreciate one of the town's historic covered bridges.

If you want an extra walk, feel free to make this stop also a reason to hike some of Koons Trail. This is totally optional, as there will be plenty of hiking opportunities at your next official stop.

Seventh Stop

Sand Bridge State Park

13180 Buffalo Rd.
Mifflinburg, PA 17844

Sand Bridge State Park is one of those places that's beautiful no matter the season. If you're up for a hike, the Bake Oven Trail is a popular choice, offering a satisfying walk through the woods without feeling overwhelming. There are plenty of other trails as well, so you can choose what fits your energy level that day.

Not feeling like hiking? You can still take in the views. The mountain overlook is an easy drive-to spot that rewards you with sweeping, north-facing panoramic views—no walking required.

Final Stop

Rusty Rail Brewing Co.

5 N 8th St Suite #1.
Mifflinburg, PA 17844

Hopefully by now you've spent enough time hiking or exploring around the park and you're ready for an early dinner...and maybe a beer or two. Rusty Rail Brewing Company is an easy, satisfying way to end your date with Mifflinburg.

Housed in a historic former rail car factory, this spot pairs local craft beer with a solid food menu and plenty of space to unwind. Whether you're debriefing the day, lingering a little longer, or just enjoying the fact that you didn't have to plan a thing, it's a fitting place to wrap things up.

Add Your Photos

Your Memory

Use this space to record
a favorite moment

Thank you for joining us on this mystery date adventure! We hope you've enjoyed the delightful experiences and memorable moments we've crafted just for you around Mifflinburg, PA.

But the adventure doesn't stop here! Keep exploring exciting mystery dates in other cities and uncover new experiences across the U.S. by visiting our website, DatesintheStates.com. There, you can purchase both physical copies and digital downloads of our mystery date books.

Plus, don't miss out on our Mystery Date Book Club, where you can receive a brand-new mystery date book every month!
Tag us in your date photos on social media! @datesinthestates

About the Creators

Crystal, the writer and creator, is a storyteller at heart. When she's not uncovering hidden gems for the next date night idea, she runs her own digital marketing company, helping small businesses improve their content marketing, increase visibility in their communities, and streamline their online presence.
Visit: crystalstatskey.com

Shane, her husband and partner in adventure, is a dedicated personal trainer and the owner of Beekstar Fitness in Irondequoit, NY. He specializes in working with clients who have limited mobility, helping them build muscle and focus on pain areas so they can regain strength and confidence in their daily lives.
Visit: beekstarfitness.com

Crystal and Shane have explored every U.S. state except Alaska (coming soon!) and are now visiting countries in alphabetical order. Whether road-tripping or curating Mystery Date experiences, they're always chasing their next adventure.

Local Love

A few local gems in the area worth exploring on your next date.

ROUPP FUNERAL HOME

HOSTS OCCASIONAL COMMUNITY EVENTS

8594 OLD TURNPIKE RD, MIFFLINBURG, PA 17844

GABLE HOUSE BAKERY

A LOCALLY LOVED BAKERY

441 CHESTNUT ST, MIFFLINBURG, PA 17844

PELICAN'S SNOBALLS

NEW ORLEANS-STYLE SHAVED ICE

104 N 8TH ST, MIFFLINBURG, PA 17844

Want to see your business here? See the next page for details on how to join!

Want to be featured?

MYSTERY DATE BOOK PACKAGES

—

Are you a small business looking to reach new customers? Feature your business in our next Mystery Date Book! Choose from our partnership packages below to connect with couples seeking unique experiences and exclusive deals.

Package One
LOCAL LOVE LISTING

—

A quick shoutout to show you're part of the neighborhood vibe.

Listed in the "Local Love" section of your designated neighborhood date book

Includes business name, address, and social link

Optional: Offer a small promo (e.g., 10% off for book holders)

1 social media shout-out when the book launches

Package Two
FEATURE STOP

—

You're not just a business— you're part of the experience.

Marked as a "Must-Stop" on a Mystery Date

Full-page feature in the book with your story, offerings and photo

Includes 1 social media feature — a dedicated post and story highlighting your business

Note: To ensure each feature is genuine and experience-based, we require a hosted visit prior to inclusion.

Package Three
PARTNER & SELLER

—

Be the spot and the source.

Everything in Tier 2

PLUS: Option to sell the Mystery Date Books at your location

Includes a bulk purchase of 10 books (yours to price + sell)

Keep 100% of the profits from in-store sales

Bonus: Have a featured "sponsored by" page and listed as an official pickup location in our promotions

Contact us for pricing. Prices subject to change.

Feel free to reach us at any time by sending us an email to say hi and to learn more! We look forward to hearing from you.

| www.datesinthestates.com | datesinthestatesblog@gmail.com |

Sponsors & Affiliates

Our sponsors and affiliates help make our adventures possible! Explore the amazing brands and businesses that support our community.

Wanderful

Wanderful is a global community for women who love to travel. Connect, explore, and join a local hub near you!

US Ghost Adventures

Take a ghost tour in one of many major US cities! Save 10% off with code: DATES10

HomeExchange

HomeExchange lets you swap homes with travelers worldwide for authentic, affordable stays. Join today and travel differently!

Loved this date? Keep the adventure going!

You can find Mystery City Date Books at select local stores near you, or visit our website for the most up-to-date list of places to purchase.

Prefer to shop online? Our online shop is open at DatesintheStates.com. You can also find our books on AbeBooks.com and Walmart.com
Just search "Mystery Date Book."

DATES IN THE STATES

A COUPLE TRAVELING THE UNITED
STATES ON A BUDGET

Contact Us

datesinthestates.com

datesinthestatesblog@gmail.com

Based in Rochester, NY

CONNECT WITH US ON SOCIAL!
@DATESINTHESTATES